CHRISTIAN VISION BOARD

Clip Art Book

for Kids

Elisa Williams

HELLO, GREAT ONE!!

Welcome to the Christian Vision Board Clip Art Book for Kids. Create an awesome prayerful and spiritual prayer vision board with this innovative clip art book.

Please leave a review because we would love your thoughts, opinions, and feedback to create better products for you!

We appreciate your support. May God bless you.

FRUITS OF THE SPIRIT

Love

joy!

PATIENCE

PEACE

generosity

Kindness

faithfulness

Gentleness

SELF CONTROL

LET THE
Word
OF
Christ
DWELL IN YOU
Richly
COLOSSIANS 3:16

FORGIVE

JESUS Loves me

HUMILITY

HOLY BIBLE HOPE

integrity

JOY

Respect

courage

e courage

Patience

Happiness

OBEDIENCE

PEACE
★ LOVE ★
JOY

THE LORD IS MY

Light

AND

Salvation

PSALM 27:1

ne, so now I say to
nmandment I give
love one another;
u, that ye also love

JESUS SAVES

PRAY

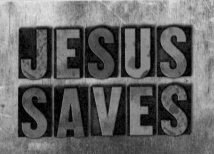
GOD

WORSHIP

GOD LOVES YOU

THANK YOU JESUS

LORD'S PRAYER

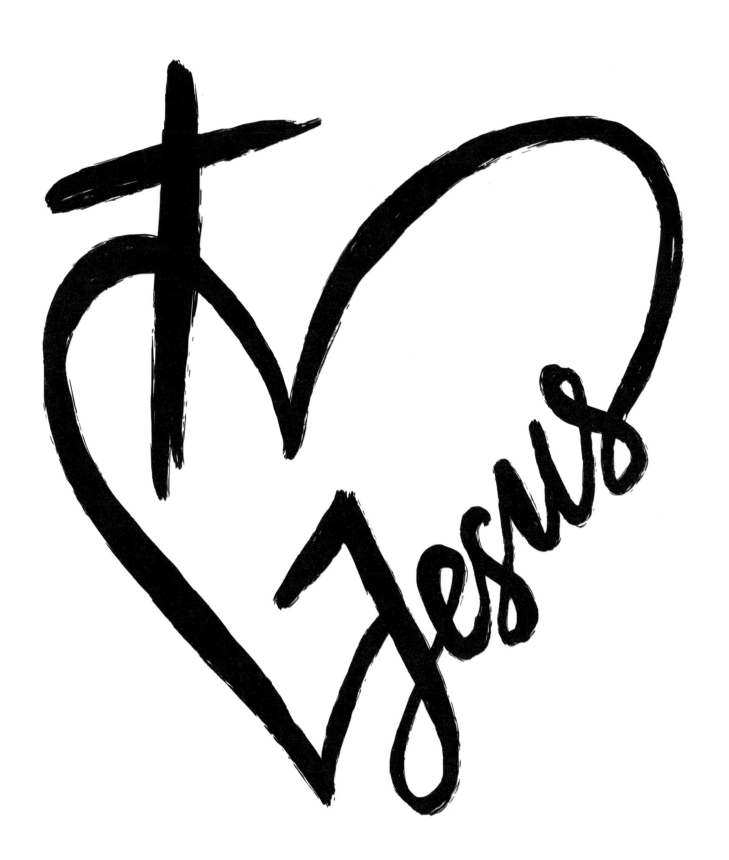

THANKSGIVING PRAYER

Dear God, thank You for this day, for my family, friends, and all the fun I had. Thank You for the food I eat and the home where I sleep. Amen.

SUPPLICATION (ASKING FOR NEEDS)

Lord, please help me with [MENTION YOUR NEED]. Give me strength, wisdom, and courage to face this and to do my best. Thank You for always listening. Amen."

THE LORD'S PRAYER

"Our Father in heaven, Hallowed be Your name. Your kingdom come, Your will be done, On earth as it is in heaven. Give us this day our daily bread.
And forgive us our debts, As we forgive our debtors.
And lead us not into temptation, But deliver us from evil.
For Yours is the kingdom and the power and the glory forever. Amen."

INTERCESSION (PRAYING FOR OTHERS)

God, please take care of [MENTION NAME]. Give them health, happiness, and Your peace. Help those in need and protect them every day. Amen.

CONFESSION PRAYER

Heavenly Father, I'm sorry for the wrong things I've done. Please forgive me for being unkind, not listening, or making bad choices. Help me to be better every day. Amen.

Jesus

IN THIS
✠ ✠
House
WE LOVE
Jesus

There is Power in Prayer

Philippians 4:6 -
"Do not be anxious about anything, but in everything by prayer and supplication with thanksgiving let your requests be made known to God."

Matthew 6:6 -
"But when you pray, go into your room, close the door and pray to your Father, who is unseen. Then your Father, who sees what is done in secret, will reward you."

2 Chronicles 7:14 -
"If my people, who are called by my name, will humble themselves and pray and seek my face and turn from their wicked ways, then I will hear from heaven, and I will forgive their sin and will heal their land."

1 Thessalonians 5:17 -
"Pray without ceasing."

Jeremiah 29:12 -
"Then you will call upon me and come and pray to me, and I will hear you."

James 5:16 -
"Therefore, confess your sins to each other and pray for each other so that you may be healed. The prayer of a righteous person is powerful and effective."

Psalm 145:18 -
"The Lord is near to all who call on him, to all who call on him in truth."

Mark 11:24 -
"Therefore I tell you, whatever you ask for in prayer, believe that you have received it, and it will be yours."

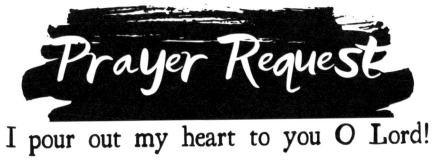

Prayer Request

I pour out my heart to you O Lord!

There Lord....

_____
_____
_____
_____
_____
_____

There Lord....

_____
_____
_____
_____
_____
_____

There Lord....

_____
_____
_____
_____
_____
_____

There Lord....

_____
_____
_____
_____
_____
_____

There Lord....

_____
_____
_____
_____
_____
_____

There Lord....

_____
_____
_____
_____
_____
_____

THERE IS POWER IN PRAYER

King Solomon's Prayer for Wisdom (1 Kings 3:9)

"Give your servant therefore an understanding mind to govern your people, that I may discern between good and evil, for who is able to govern this your great people?"

The Prayer of Jabez (1 Chronicles 4:10)

"Oh, that you would bless me indeed and enlarge my territory, that Your hand would be with me, and that You would keep me from evil, that I may not cause pain!"

The Serenity Prayer by Reinhold Niebuhr

"God, grant me the serenity to accept the things I cannot change, courage to change the things I can, and wisdom to know the difference.

David's Prayer of Repentance (Psalm 51:10-12)

"Create in me a clean heart, O God, and renew a right spirit within me. Cast me not away from your presence, and take not your Holy Spirit from me. Restore to me the joy of your salvation, and uphold me with a willing spirit."

Mother Teresa's Prayer

"Lord, lead me, guide me, walk beside me, help me find the way. Teach me all that I must do to live with you someday."

St. Francis of Assisi's Prayer

"Lord, make me an instrument of your peace: where there is hatred, let me sow love; where there is injury, pardon; where there is doubt, faith; where there is despair, hope; where there is darkness, light; where there is sadness, joy."

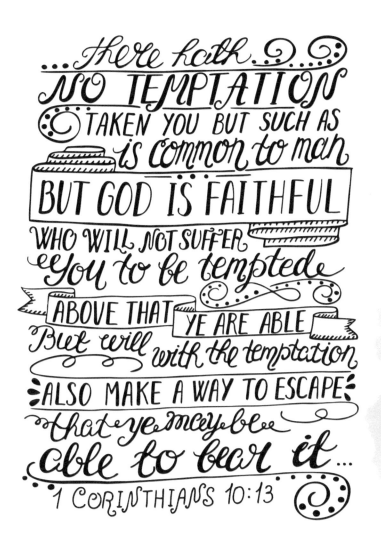

...there hath NO TEMPTATION TAKEN YOU BUT SUCH AS is common to man BUT GOD IS FAITHFUL WHO WILL NOT SUFFER you to be tempted ABOVE THAT YE ARE ABLE But will with the temptation ALSO MAKE A WAY TO ESCAPE that ye may be able to bear it ... 1 CORINTHIANS 10:13

You are FEARFULLY AND WONDERFULLY made PSALM 139:14

a Godliness WITH Contentment is GREAT GAIN 1 Timothy 6:6

LET the little CHILDREN come to Me • MARK 10·14 •

I'M CHILD of God

I CAN DO
All things
THROUGH CHRIST
which strengtheneth
me
· Philippians 4·13 ·

CASTING
all
YOUR CARE
upon
H·I·M
for
HE CARETH
for you
1 PETER 5:7

blessed
&
loved

Bless
THIS
child

BEFORE
you
WERE
born
I SET YOU
apart
JEREMIAH 1:5

Faith
CAN MOVE
MOUNTAINS

Be careful
FOR
NOTHING
but
IN EVERY THING
by prayer and
supplication
WITH THANKSGIVING
LET YOUR REQUESTS
be made known
UNTO G·O·D
Philippians 4:6

FAITH IS
GOD
CHANGES
Everything

WHERE GOD
Guides
HE
PROVIDES

child
OF
God

not TODAY
Satan

all things
WORK
TOGETHER
FOR
GOOD
to
THEM THAT
love
G·O·D

God is
GOOD
all the time

GIVE IT TO
God
AND GO TO
Sleep

Jesus
IS
Life

ALWAYS
be
Joyful

GOD
faith
SUCCESS

Blessed
AND
love

ANCHORED IN CHRIST

SUCCESS

REDEEMED BY GRACE

I LOVE JESUS

AMEN!

God is Love

TO GOD BE THE GLORY

grateful

THANK YOU GOD FOR MY FAMILY

THANK YOU FOR MY HEALTH

JESUS NEVER FAILS

Blessed

"BUT THE LORD IS FAITHFUL, AND HE WILL STRENGTHEN YOU AND PROTECT YOU FROM THE EVIL ONE." (2 THESSALONIANS 3:3)

"GO INTO ALL THE WORLD AND PREACH THE GOSPEL TO ALL CREATION." (MARK 16:15)

"The Lord will keep you from all harm—He will watch over your life." (Psalm 121:7)

"I can do all things through Christ who strengthens me." (Philippians 4:13)

WWW.CAPITOLCITYCHRISTIAN.ORG
WE LOVE BECAUSE HE FIRST LOVED US
1 JOHN 4:19

JESUS is my ROCK

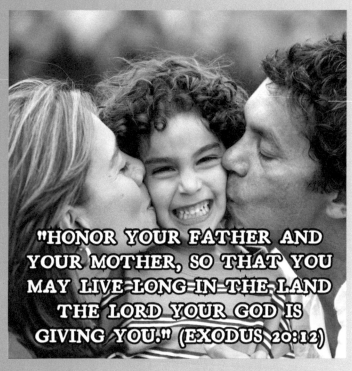

"HONOR YOUR FATHER AND YOUR MOTHER, SO THAT YOU MAY LIVE LONG IN THE LAND THE LORD YOUR GOD IS GIVING YOU." (EXODUS 20:12)

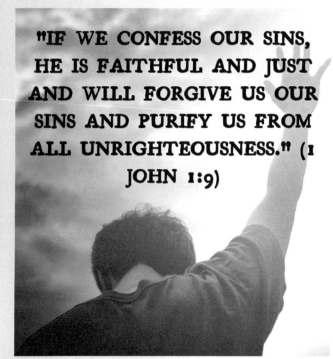

"IF WE CONFESS OUR SINS, HE IS FAITHFUL AND JUST AND WILL FORGIVE US OUR SINS AND PURIFY US FROM ALL UNRIGHTEOUSNESS." (1 JOHN 1:9)

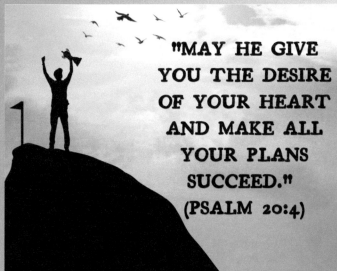

"MAY HE GIVE YOU THE DESIRE OF YOUR HEART AND MAKE ALL YOUR PLANS SUCCEED." (PSALM 20:4)

"COMMIT TO THE LORD WHATEVER YOU DO, AND HE WILL ESTABLISH YOUR PLANS." (PROVERBS 16:3)

EXERCISE YOUR FAITH WALK WITH JESUS

I WILL WALK BY faith EVEN WHEN I can not see

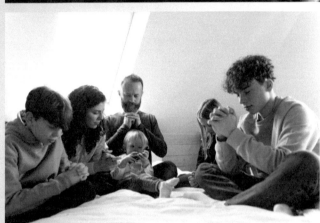

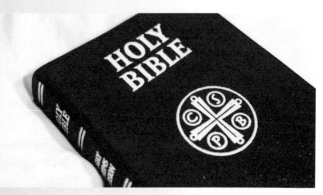

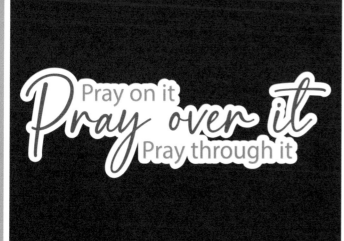

Prayer Request

I pour out my heart to you O Lord!

There Lord....

_____
_____
_____
_____
_____
_____

There Lord....

_____
_____
_____
_____
_____
_____

There Lord....

_____
_____
_____
_____
_____
_____

There Lord....

_____
_____
_____
_____
_____
_____

There Lord....

_____
_____
_____
_____
_____

There Lord....

_____
_____
_____
_____
_____

Made in the USA
Columbia, SC
13 February 2025

53771862R00024